FRANCIS FRITH'S

AROUND THE
KENT COAST

PHOTOGRAPHIC MEMORIES

GEOFFREY BUTLER has had a shop in the Pantiles for thirty years. He has always had a deep interest in the Pantiles and the Common, and has written accounts of several aspects of Pantiles history. He is also a conservator for the Common.

KEITH HETHERINGTON is a retired craftsman with an electricity supply company. He has written many articles for the monthly magazine *Bygone Kent*. He is the author of *Old Pubs of Tunbridge Wells and District* and *Yesterday's Bottles*, and co-author of *The Pantiles Guide*.

FRANCIS FRITH'S
PHOTOGRAPHIC MEMORIES

AROUND THE KENT COAST

PHOTOGRAPHIC MEMORIES

GEOFFREY BUTLER
AND KEITH HETHERINGTON

First published in the United Kingdom in 2005 by
The Francis Frith Collection®

Hardback Edition 2005
ISBN 1-85937-665-7

British Library Cataloguing in Publication Data

Around the Kent Coast - Photographic Memories
Geoffrey Butler and Keith Hetherington
ISBN 1-85937-665-7

The Francis Frith Collection®
Frith's Barn, Teffont,
Salisbury, Wiltshire SP3 5QP
Tel: +44 (0) 1722 716 376
Email: info@francisfrith.co.uk
www.francisfrith.co.uk

Printed and bound in Great Britain

Front Cover: **RAMSGATE**, *The Beach 1907* 58272
Frontispiece: **FOLKESTONE,** *Lower Landgate Road Toll
        Gate 1927* 80387

*The colour-tinting is for illustrative purposes only, and is not intended to be
historically accurate*

AS WITH ANY HISTORICAL DATABASE THE FRITH ARCHIVE IS
CONSTANTLY BEING CORRECTED AND IMPROVED AND THE
PUBLISHERS WOULD WELCOME INFORMATION ON OMISSIONS
OR INACCURACIES

CONTENTS

FRANCIS FRITH
VICTORIAN PIONEER

FRANCIS FRITH, founder of the world-famous photographic archive, was a complex and multi-talented man. A devout Quaker and a highly successful Victorian businessman, he was philosophical by nature and pioneering in outlook.

By 1855 he had already established a wholesale grocery business in Liverpool, and sold it for the astonishing sum of £200,000, which is the equivalent today of over £15,000,000. Now a very rich man, he was able to indulge his passion for travel. As a child he had pored over travel books written by early explorers, and his fancy and imagination had been stirred by family holidays to the sublime mountain regions of Wales and Scotland. 'What lands of spirit-stirring and enriching scenes and places!' he had written. He was to return to these scenes of grandeur in later years to 'recapture the thousands of vivid and tender memories', but with a different purpose. Now in his thirties, and captivated by the new science of photography, Frith set out on a series of pioneering journeys up the Nile and to the

Near East that occupied him from 1856 until 1860.

INTRIGUE AND EXPLORATION

These far-flung journeys were packed with intrigue and adventure. In his life story, written when he was sixty-three, Frith tells of being held captive by bandits, and of fighting 'an awful midnight battle to the very point of surrender with a deadly pack of hungry, wild dogs'. Wearing flowing Arab costume, Frith arrived at Akaba by camel sixty years before Lawrence of Arabia, where he encountered 'desert princes and rival sheikhs, blazing with jewel-hilted swords'.

He was the first photographer to venture beyond the sixth cataract of the Nile. Africa was still the mysterious 'Dark Continent', and Stanley and Livingstone's historic meeting was a decade into the future. The conditions for picture taking confound belief. He laboured for hours in his wicker dark-room in the sweltering heat of the desert, while the volatile chemicals fizzed dangerously in their trays. Back in London he exhibited his photographs and was 'rapturously cheered' by members of the Royal Society. His reputation as a photographer was made overnight.

VENTURE OF A LIFE-TIME

Characteristically, Frith quickly spotted the opportunity to create a new business as a specialist publisher of photographs. He lived in an era of immense and sometimes violent change.

For the poor in the early part of Victoria's reign work was exhausting and the hours long, and people had precious little free time to enjoy themselves. Most had no transport other than a cart or gig at their disposal, and rarely travelled far beyond the boundaries of their own town or village. However, by the 1870s the railways had threaded their way across the country, and Bank Holidays and half-day Saturdays had been made obligatory by Act of Parliament. All of a sudden the working man and his family were able to enjoy days out and see a little more of the world.

With typical business acumen, Francis Frith foresaw that these new tourists would enjoy having souvenirs to commemorate their days out. In 1860 he married Mary Ann Rosling and set out on a new career: his aim was to photograph every city, town and village in Britain. For the next thirty years he travelled the country by train and by pony and trap, producing fine photographs of seaside resorts and beauty spots that were keenly bought by millions of Victorians. These prints were painstakingly pasted into family albums and pored over during the dark nights of winter, rekindling precious memories of summer excursions.

THE RISE OF FRITH & CO

Frith's studio was soon supplying retail shops all over the country. To meet the demand he gathered about him a small team of photographers, and published the work of independent artist-photographers of the calibre of Roger Fenton and Francis Bedford. In order to gain some understanding of the scale of Frith's business one only has to look at the catalogue issued by Frith & Co in 1886: it runs to some 670 pages, listing not only many thousands of views of the British Isles but also many photographs of most European countries, and China, Japan, the USA and Canada - note the sample page shown on page 9 from the hand-written Frith & Co ledgers recording the pictures. By 1890 Frith had created the greatest specialist photographic publishing company in the world, with over 2,000 sales outlets - more than the combined number that Boots and WH Smith have today! The picture on the next page shows the Frith & Co display board at Ingleton in the Yorkshire Dales (left of window). Beautifully constructed with a mahogany frame and gilt inserts, it could display up to a dozen local scenes.

POSTCARD BONANZA

The ever-popular holiday postcard we know today took many years to develop. In 1870 the Post Office issued the first plain cards, with a pre-printed stamp on one face. In 1894 they allowed other publishers' cards to be sent through the mail with an attached adhesive halfpenny stamp. Demand grew rapidly, and in 1895 a new size of postcard was permitted called the court card, but there was little room for illustration. In 1899, a year after Frith's death, a new card measuring 5.5 x 3.5 inches became the standard format, but it was not until 1902 that the divided back came into being, so that the address and message could be on one face and a full-size illustration on the other. Frith & Co were in the vanguard of postcard development: Frith's sons Eustace and Cyril continued their father's monumental task, expanding the number of views offered to the public and recording more and more places in Britain, as the

5	•	*...College, View from the Gardens*					
6	•	*St Catherine's College*		+	+		
7	•	*Senate House Library*		+			
8	•			+			
9	•	*Gerrard Hostel Bridge*		+	+		
3 0	•	*Geological Museum*		+	+	+	+
1	•	*Addenbrooke's Hospital*			+		
2	•	*St Mary's Church*			+		
3	•	*Fitzwilliam Museum, Pitt Press &c*			+		
4	•						
5	*Buxton, The Crescent*				+		
6	*The Colonnade*				+		
7	*Public Gardens*				+		
8					+		
9	*Haddon Hall, View from the Terrace*				+		
4 0	*Miller's Dale*				+		

coasts and countryside were opened up to mass travel.

Francis Frith had died in 1898 at his villa in Cannes, his great project still growing. The archive he created continued in business for another seventy years. By 1970 it contained over a third of a million pictures showing 7,000 British towns and villages.

FRANCIS FRITH'S LEGACY

Frith's legacy to us today is of immense significance and value, for the magnificent archive of evocative photographs he created provides a unique record of change in the cities, towns and villages throughout Britain over a century and more. Frith and his fellow studio photographers revisited locations many times down the years to update their views, compiling for us an enthralling and colourful pageant of British life and character.

We are fortunate that Frith was dedicated to recording the minutiae of everyday life. For it is this sheer wealth of visual data, the painstaking chronicle of changes in dress, transport, street layouts, buildings, housing, engineering and landscape that captivates us so much today. His remarkable images offer us a powerful link with the past and with the lives of our ancestors.

THE VALUE OF THE ARCHIVE TODAY

Computers have now made it possible for Frith's many thousands of images to be accessed almost instantly. Frith's images are increasingly used as visual resources, by social historians, by researchers into genealogy and ancestry, by architects and town planners, and by teachers involved in local history projects.

In addition, the archive offers every one of us an opportunity to examine the places where we and our families have lived and worked down the years. Highly successful in Frith's own era, the archive is now, a century and more on, entering a new phase of popularity. Historians consider the Francis Frith Collection to be of prime national importance. It is the only archive of its kind remaining in private ownership. Francis Frith's archive is now housed in an historic timber barn in the beautiful village of Teffont in Wiltshire. Its founder would not recognize the archive office as it is today. In place of the many thousands of dusty boxes containing glass plate negatives and an all-pervading odour of photographic chemicals, there are now ranks of computer screens. He would be amazed to watch his images travelling round the world at unimaginable speeds through internet lines.

The archive's future is both bright and exciting. Francis Frith, with his unshakeable belief in making photographs available to the greatest number of people, would undoubtedly approve of what is being done today with his lifetime's work. His photographs depicting our shared past are now bringing pleasure and enlightenment to millions around the world a century and more after his death.

AROUND THE KENT COAST
AN INTRODUCTION

THE KENT COAST has been the scene of many changes. The erosion of the sea has created its own landscape - the prime example and one of the most famous areas is Romney Marshes. This area is easily accessible, but it remains a strange terrain intersected by dykes, providing some of the best soil and sheep grazing in the country. The area was originally a forest, but it was submerged by the sea. Over the centuries has been drained and reclaimed, but it still retains the character of a flat boundless space. The various attempts at drainage forced the shingle to accumulate at Dungeness, which has given the area a unique shingle beach, probably the longest beach of its type in Europe. As the sea retreats, so the beach retains more shingle, and this has resulted in a succession of lighthouses being built.

One result of the constant erosion is that one hundred yards from the beach the sea is sixty feet deep, and ships can pass quite safely near to the shore. Probably because of this natural sea depth, nuclear power stations were built at Dungeness between 1965 and 1968; the water is drawn from the deep channels for cooling and then returned to the sea after use.

As we follow the coast the shingle turns to sand, but the erosion of the sea has stranded towns such as Lydd and New Romney. There are sand dunes at Greatstone on Sea, and the sand continues along the coast. At Dymchurch the sea is always a constant threat, and a huge sea wall keeps the sea from the main road. Passing by Hythe, the sea emerges at Sandgate, where it runs parallel with the road and gives a wonderful introduction to the white cliffs at Folkestone and Dover. These cliffs date back to the Jurassic era, and in the Warren, which runs alongside the cliffs at Folkestone, many fossils of sea creatures can be found in the chalk. The area is also a nature reserve, and supports many rare plants and wildlife.

Between Folkestone and Dover is the entrance to the Channel Tunnel at Cheriton. The tunnel runs under the chalk cliffs at Folkestone, then deep under the Channel to Sangatte near Calais. Work on the tunnel started in 1988 and finished in 1998. The workings excavated from the tunnel were transferred to a site near Dover, where it forms a convincing chalk cliff coastline. This area is called Samphire Hoe, and was named after the edible herb, samphire, which is found here. Samphire Hoe is now a nature reserve, where many rare chalk plants grow; they attract a wealth of butterflies and other insects, and seasonal migratory birds. The area is open to visitors, and has some good accessible paths.

From Dover the cliffs extend through St Margaret's Bay and end at Kingsdown. The coast then continues through Walmer and Deal, but bypasses Sandwich. Sandwich was once one of the main ports, but it is now over a mile inland owing to the silting up of the River Stour. We go on via Pegwell Bay to the Isle of Thanet. Thanet was once a natural island separated from the mainland by the Wantsum Channel but this has now completely silted up, making the area part of the mainland. On the Isle of Thanet are the popular holiday resorts of Ramsgate, Margate and Broadstairs.

As the coast continues, the geological structure changes: from Reculver onwards, London clay appears. This relatively soft material causes the coastline to be constantly changing, and many traces of early settlements have been found in this area. London clay is an Eocene deposit, and in this clay there is a wealth of fossils. As the coast continues through Herne Bay, there is an unusual feature near Whitstable at Tankerton. Here there is a natural breakwater called 'The Street': this has been caused by a huge bank of clay, which has become impregnated with a layer of shingle. The bank runs for half a mile out to sea, but it is only accessible at low tide. The Street is a natural hunting ground for fossil shark's teeth and iron pyrites nodules.

The coast continues through Whitstable with its famous oyster beds to the Isle of Sheppey, now connected to the mainland by a new bridge. The coastline is once again London clay, and at various points on the north coast it is possible to find fossils on the beach. Warden's Point and Leysdown on Sea are particularly good areas; both have London clay cliffs, but the cliffs can be very treacherous in wet weather, and the beach is only accessible at low tide. Fossils found in this area include shark's teeth, crayfish and crab, and septarian nodules, a mixture of mudstone and calcite which can contain carbonised wood with teredo (shipworm) borings.

The Hoo Peninsula juts out between two great rivers, the Thames on the west and the Medway on the east. The Thames has completed its journey from London, whilst the Medway winds through Rochester and Chatham on its way to the sea. The Hoo Peninsula is fairly flat, but it does have hills and a wooded area. At Cliffe there is a vast marsh, home to many sea birds, both common and rare. The area has been discussed as a possible site for a new airfield, but the local residents have fiercely opposed the scheme, as it would mean the destruction of the sea bird sanctuary as well as the loss of several coastal villages. At the far end of the peninsula is the Isle of Grain, now taken over by British Petroleum for the storage of oil. Although the Hoo Peninsula is a very quiet area, it is still well worth a visit.

Practically every village and town on the Kent coast is proud of its heritage, and many towns have reminders of the past. The coast has always been in the forefront of the defence of the country, and the white cliffs of Dover have always symbolised Britain's determination to repel invaders. Around the Kent coast there is tangible evidence of how people of every period from the

Romans onwards have fortified the coasts.

From the earliest times traces of ancient man have been found in many places, and Bronze Age artefacts have been found at Reculver. There are traces of very early hill defences at Folkestone, and remains of Roman forts can be found at Reculver, Richborough, Lympne and Dover. The Norman Conquest initiated extensive castle building; the prime example stands proud and dominant at Dover.

The chalk cliffs between Dover and Folkestone represented a natural obstacle to invasion, but as Dover was the nearest point to the continent, it was a prize target. In spite of the protection of the cliffs, it always needed to be heavily fortified. Sandwich Bay offered a superb landing site, and this was particularly useful in the 17th and 18th centuries for smuggling.

The next extensive round of fortification took place during the reign of Henry VIII in the 16th century, when more defences were built in Kent than in any other county. Castles were planned and built at Walmer, Deal and Sandgate, and new defences were erected at Dover.

During the Napoleonic wars of the 19th century, the threat to the Kent coast became even more apparent. Sturdy brick towers called Martello towers, each capable of holding defensive guns, were built along the Kent coast; 27 towers were built, of which 16 survive. Examples can be seen at Folkestone, Hythe and Dymchurch. In addition, a military canal was constructed from Hythe to Winchelsea in Sussex, and this waterway can be seen on the journey to Hythe. The canal's function was to be an obstacle for invaders and also a means to transport goods, supplies and troops. In the 19th century, a fort was built at Cliffe near Dover, which still remains.

World War I again saw the Kent coast in the forefront of the hostilities. Air raids both by Zeppelin and Gotha bombers were centred on Folkestone and Herne Bay, and fighter airfields were established near the coast at Manston and Hawkinge to aid in the defence of the region. World War II saw Dover once more in the centre of the defence of the country. The shipping passing in the Channel needed constant protection from both the Stuka dive bombers and also from the constant shelling from the French coast. Gun emplacements were built on the cliffs, but the town was a prime target for ground attack aircraft. Folkestone and other towns also suffered from air activity, mainly in the form of daylight raids. Massive preparations were made against an attempted invasion: a line of defence was constructed between Dover and Whitstable, and another line along the bank of the Royal Military Canal. Traces of these defences, including pillboxes, can be seen at Folkestone and along the canal. Luckily, these defences were not needed, and now the airfield at Manston is a civil airport, whilst the airfield at Hawkinge no longer exists.

With the Channel Tunnel and the creation of the EEC, it is to be hoped that the Kent coast as a defensive zone will no longer be necessary. But one danger remains, a legacy of the 17th and 18th century – smuggling.

In 1698 a law was passed forbidding the buying and selling of wool within 15 miles of the coast which was to be enforced by a corps of Riding Officers. As there was considerable demand for wool on the Continent, this law was soon broken; the offence was called 'owling'.

Wool was smuggled by sea into France in exchange for contraband. Numerous gangs operated within Kent at Folkestone, St Margaret's Bay and Dymchurch. At Dymchurch, the Ship Inn (which still survives) was famous for its association with smugglers. The author Russell Thorndike based his famous character Doctor Syn in Dymchurch and the Romney Marshes. In 1724 duty was levied on tea, which could be smuggled from France and sold in London at three times the price. In 1746 a huge consignment of tea was landed at Sandwich Bay. The gangs controlling the smuggling fell out, and this led to a pitched battle on the sands. In 1751 further controls were levied on gin and tobacco; it was estimated that one third of the gin consumed was smuggled in. These controls, and a further duty on tea, caused an increase in smuggling. The war with France did not stop the smugglers' trade, but the concentration of troops along the Kent coast made it more difficult.

In 1820 a landing was carried out close to Sandgate Castle involving 300 smugglers, and this led to a pitched battle with the Excise men. Because of the security structure at Dover, the town was not too involved in the smuggling of the 17th and 18th centuries, but the opening in the 20th century of the Channel Tunnel has brought the Dover area into the forefront of contraband smuggling and the traffic in refugees.

Owing to the long and fascinating history of the Kent coast, most of the towns and villages along the coast respect their heritage, and they are proud to display their own particular landmarks. As you go along the coast, there are many historic places to visit, nature reserves, and signposted coastal walks.

The coast has also been the residence of many famous authors, including Charles Dickens, who lived at Broadstairs, where an annual Dickens festival is held. Dickens also lived at Higham on the Hoo Peninsula, and Cooling church was his inspiration for the churchyard scene in *Great Expectations*. Ian Fleming, who wrote the James Bond novels, lived at St Margaret's Bay, and Edith Nesbitt, who wrote *The Railway Children* and many other children's books, lived at Dymchurch and later at St Mary's Bay. Other famous authors include John Buchan, who lived at Broadstairs, H G Wells, who lived at Sandgate, and Noel Coward, who lived in a converted stable at St Mary's Bay. There are many more authors who have lived on the coast, and who must have found it a peaceful and inspiring place for their craft.

Another unusual feature of the coast is the Romney, Hythe and Dymchurch Railway, a one-third size replica steam train that runs from Hythe to Dungeness. It has thirteen and a half miles of track and is open all summer and at weekends in the winter. There are so many other attractions along the coast that it is difficult to single out any particular place - the whole coast line is full of fascinating places - please pay it a visit.

AROUND THE KENT COAST

ALLHALLOWS, *Beatty Cottages c1955* A229004

Allhallows on the Hoo Peninsula is a small village that at the peak of its popularity could attract up to 10,000 visitors at Bank Holidays. There was a railway link from 1935 until it closed in 1961. The whole village was put under threat when the government proposed a new airport at Cliffe in 2003, which would mean the end of Allhallows village.

ALLHALLOWS
The Camping Site
c1955 A229022

Following World War II, most families looked forward to a week at the seaside, which would often be in a caravan, and on sites similar to this one.

BIRCHINGTON, *The Square c1955* B278002

Birchington is three miles west of Margate. The artist and poet Dante Gabriel Rossetti lived here until his death in 1882, and he was interred in All Saints' churchyard. The drinking fountain in the centre of this photograph was given to the town by R Grant JP in memory of his wife. On the left is Lloyds Bank, Jenner's Garage, the Smugglers Café and, most important, a fish and chip shop.

▼ **BROADSTAIRS,** *St Mary's Home 1891* 29411

St Mary's Home in Stone Road was a convalescent home and orphanage for children, with a Miss Brimble as the secretary.

▶ **BROADSTAIRS**
The Sands 1902 48841

Once known as 'Bradstow', Broadstairs was a fishing village that grew to be one of the most popular Kent seaside towns. Note the bathing tents, and local boats on the right.

◄ **BROADSTAIRS**
The Beach 1912
65019

This is Main Bay, which changed its name to Viking Bay following the arrival in 1949 of a replica Viking ship, the *Hugin*. This ship was built to celebrate the 1500th anniversary of the landing of Hengist and Horsa and the incursions into Britain of the Anglo-Saxons and Danes. The boat had been rowed to Broadstairs from Denmark.

► **BROADSTAIRS**
The White Cliffs 1918 68481

The low white cliffs at Broadstairs shelter this bay, and people are making use of the tents on the beach to change for a dip in the sea.

BROADSTAIRS
*The Bandstand and
the Promenade 1907*
58329

Just below the promenade
and overlooked by some
prominent hotels, these
visitors enjoy a sunny day.
The feeling of the time
was that ladies should
cover up, so parasols keep
the sun at bay.

► **BROADSTAIRS**
The Beach 1918
68482

A large crowd is
gathered on the beach
in the centre of this
photograph, possibly
to watch a Punch and
Judy show; these
shows had become
very popular beach
entertainments from
the 19th century.

◄ **BROADSTAIRS**
*The Promenade and
the Gardens 1918*
68483

On the left is the Albion
Hotel, where Charles
Dickens stayed before he
bought the property
overlooking the bay on the
right of the photograph. It
was known as Fort House,
and Dickens lived there in
1851. Dickens loved this
house, and called it his
'airy nest'; it was here that
he wrote *David
Copperfield*. Today the
property is known as Bleak
House, after another book
by Dickens.

▲ **CLIFFE,** *The View from the Church c1955* C464009

Once known as 'Coveshoo', Cliffe was a meeting place for the Great Councils of Kent in Saxon times. The ridge top village of Cliffe was constantly in the news during 2003, when the villagers and other local people fought a vigorous campaign against the government's proposed siting of a new airport at Cliffe. They were supported by the RSPB, who said that an airport here would mean an end to the wildlife reserves nearby.

◄**CLIFFE**
Church Street c1955
C464022

Sometimes called Cliffe at Hoo, the area is known today for its Portland cement works and chalk quarries. On the left of this photograph stands The Six Bells public house, which was one of the properties of the Maidstone brewers Style & Winch Ltd. Two landlords of the pub were John Jenkins and John Topley. In the centre is Parker & Son, a grocer's and general stores.

► **CLIFFE**
Church Street c1955
C464024

On the right is the Cliffe post office, with a pillar box outside. The Black Bull pub (centre) was another property of the Maidstone brewers Style & Winch. This fully licensed house later featured exotic food from the Far East. Note the weatherboarded houses, so typical of Kent.

◄ **COOLING CASTLE**
The Gateway c1960
C466029

Cooling Castle was built in the 14th century, and was once owned by Sir John Oldcastle, on whom Shakespeare based his character Falstaff. Today it is the home of musician and TV presenter Jools Holland.

◄ BROADSTAIRS
*The North Foreland
Lighthouse c1965*
B220032

This lighthouse was
built in the late 17th
century. It was
heightened in the 18th
century, and then
lowered one hundred
years later.

◄ BROADSTAIRS
Viking Bay c1955
B220054

On the top of the low cliffs
are (from the right) the
Marchesi Brothers'
restaurant, the Albion
Hotel, the Victoria
Restaurant, and Blades
guest house. The town
holds an annual Dickens
festival when people dress
up in Victorian costumes
and listen to readings from
Dickens's books.

► **BROADSTAIRS**
The View from the Cliffe c1960
B220077

We are looking from the Cliffe; Bleak House is prominent in the centre of the photograph. Note the small train ride in the left-hand corner of the beach. Former Prime Minister Edward Heath lived at Broadstairs, and so did the round-the-world yachtsman Alec Rose. Sailing at Broadstairs has always been very popular.

◄ **CHERITON**
The Schools 1902
48836

Cheriton had two National Schools; one for boys was built in 1869 for 100 pupils, and the other school, for 150 girls and infants, was built in 1887.

▲ **DEAL,** *From the Pier Pavilion 1899* 44203

Two kiosks at the entrance to the pier used to take bookings for cruises and shows. On the right of the pier are two of the town's hotels, The Antwerp and The Clarendon. The pier has always been popular with fishermen, and catches of bass, bull huss, cod, conger, dab, dogfish, flounder, mullet, plaice, pouting and sole are common.

◀**DEAL**
From the Pier 1899
44204

The tall building with a flag flying at the top (right) was the Beach House Temperance Hotel. Further along is the Timeball Tower (centre), built to give Greenwich Mean Time to passing ships by dropping a large ball down a shaft at the top of the tower at exactly 1pm every day. It operated from 1855 until 1927.

▼ **DEAL,** *The Castle 1894* 34217

The castle was built in 1539, and came under the control of the Lord Warden of the Cinque Ports. In 1648 the castle was captured by Colonel Nathaniel Rich for Parliament. The white building to the rear of the castle has been demolished.

▶ **DEAL**
Sandown Castle 1906
56924

Sandown Castle once stood at the northern end of Deal. These ruins are all that remain of the castle erected by Henry VIII; they were purchased by the corporation in 1894.

◄ **DEAL**
*The Bandstand
1924* 76055

The bandstand was situated near the Timeball Tower. Here, it displays a poster which advertises a military band concert by the East Surrey Regiment. A few people enjoy the concert from the comfort of the many deckchairs set out for them. The bandstand was later moved to Walmer.

► **DEAL**
The Pier c1955
D15087

The iron pier was opened in 1864. During World War II it was badly damaged when it was struck by a Dutch motor vessel. In 1957 the Duke of Edinburgh opened the present pier. William Cobbett came through Deal in 1823, and in his *Rural Rides* he said that he had found it 'a villainous place, full of filthy looking people.'

▶ **DOVER**
The Castle 1887
19981

The castle at Dover was built between 1181 and 1187 by Henry II. A Roman stone lighthouse, the Pharos, stands in the castle grounds near the Saxon church of St Mary in Castro. Also within the grounds are the underground passages and caves used for shelter and military purposes during the last war.

◀ **DOVER**
St Radigund's Abbey and Farmhouse 1891
29676

The 12th-century St Radigund's Abbey is at Alkham. At one time it was an important abbey, but now it is an ivy-covered ruin and part of a farm.

▲ **DOVER,** *The Grand Hotel 1892* 31420

Some fine hotels were built in Victorian times to cater for the wealthy visitors to the town, such as the Grand Hotel that faced Granville Gardens.

◄**DOVER**
General View 1899
44795

Dover was the chief Cinque Port, and the white cliffs were the first sight of England for visitors arriving by boat. Known as the 'Gateway to England', Dover makes an impressive image for visitors, with its castle dominating the skyline. The pier on the right had wooden landing stages for pleasure cruisers.

29

DOVER, *From Belle Vue Tea Gardens 1901* 48057

At the time of this photograph, Dover had two docks, Granville Dock and Wellington Dock, and two piers, Admiralty Pier (built in 1848), and Promenade Pier (built in 1893 and demolished in 1927). The harbour came under the control of the Dover Harbour Board in 1923, which developed it into one of the busiest ports in the world.

DOVER
Admiralty Pier 1901
48059

Admiralty Pier was constructed from a small jetty called Cheesmans Head in 1848, and it was enlarged and altered over the years. The boat trains that used it were run by the Southern Railway and the London, Chatham and Dover Railway. The most famous train to make the run was the *Golden Arrow*, which made its last journey to the docks on 30 September 1972. Dover now handles large cruise ships, and one of its terminals is still decorated with Southern Railway livery.

DOVER, *The Promenade 1908* 60393

In Roman times Dover was known as Dubris. One of the premier hotels was The Grand, which can be seen behind the seated woman with the white parasol (left). Dover was known as 'Hellfire Corner' in the last war, as it was bombed and shelled and many buildings were destroyed.

DOVER
The Promenade 1908
60396

The busy Dover promenade was very popular with visitors; a pier was added to it in 1893 at a cost of £28,000. Behind the boat with sails up (centre left) we can just see a row of bathing machines, which could be towed down to the water so that the bathers could step out of the machine straight into the sea.

DUNGENESS
The New Lighthouse
c1960 D165015

On 29 June 1960 the Duke of Gloucester, the Master of Trinity House, opened the first new lighthouse to be built in Britain for 50 years. It was built on the site of the old fog signal at Dungeness.

DUNGENESS, *The Lighthouse c1955* D165022

The first lighthouse at Dungeness was built in 1610, and lit by a coal fire. It was replaced in 1792 by a lighthouse lit by sperm whale oil. In 1904 the lighthouse in this photograph was built, with an incandescent paraffin light that could be seen for twenty miles.

DYMCHURCH
Main Road 1903
50384

Dymchurch lies seven feet below the high water mark, and is protected by the Dymchurch Wall; there has been a protective wall here since Roman times. Dymchurch was the meeting place of the Lords of the Level who looked after the drainage of the Romney Marshes. The quiet street scene in the photograph is a far cry from the busy holiday traffic of today.

DYMCHURCH, *1921* 71105

Dymchurch has always had a strong connection with smugglers, and this was the basis of the stories of the mythical Dr Syn, a smuggling parson, by Russell Thorndike. The people of the area supported the smugglers. On one occasion, when a captured smuggler was being escorted through Dymchurch by a revenue man, the locals threw stones at the revenue man until he was forced to release his prisoner. Dymchurch, a small town consisting of one street on the road from New Romney to Hythe, was once a place of some importance. It had a charter granted to it by Edward IV, and confirmed by both Edward IV and James I

▼ **DYMCHURCH,** *The War Memorial 1921* 71109

In front of the church is the Dymchurch war memorial, erected in 1921 in memory of the men of Dymchurch who fell in the Great War 1914-1918.

▶ **DYMCHURCH**
The Sands 1927 80397

Dymchurch has built up a reputation as a children's paradise because of its sands and its fun fair. In this photograph children survey the pool of water for crabs, and a father is building a sandcastle. In the background is the Sea View Tea Room.

◄ **DYMCHURCH**
The Beach and the Promenade 1927
80399

Note the old telephone poles on the left. The defensive wall runs for three miles, and had to be repaired following the tidal surge in 1953.

► **DYMCHURCH**
The High Street c1955
D74004

On the left of this photograph of the High Street is the boarded-up shop of E Wraight, cycle agent. The Wraight brothers were also builders, blacksmiths and undertakers. Next door is the Gift Shop, and across the road is J A Norman, selling fruit and vegetables. Also in the High Street was the Ship Inn, which had a very strong connection with smugglers. The Lords, Bailiff and Jurats of Romney Marsh used to hold their annual lunch there, and turned a blind eye to any smuggling activities.

DYMCHURCH
The Car Park and the Fun Fair c1955 D74006

A busy funfair surrounds the Martello Tower. This one was number 24 of 103 built along the south coast in the early 1800s as a defence against a possible invasion by Napoleon. It has been restored and opened to the public.

▶ **DYMCHURCH**
The Beach looking East c1955 D74008

Visitors enjoy the beach at Dymchurch whilst a boat waits to take people on a cruise. In days gone by, this beach would have witnessed the landing of contraband; here the local smugglers would exchange wool and live sheep for their goods.

◀ **DYMCHURCH**
The Shop on the Sea Wall c1965 D74037

Here we see a typical family trip to the seaside. The boy has his bucket and spade, the girl a bucket, and dad has his pipe. The old boathouse is selling beach balls, lilos, straw hats and so on, but most important from the parents' point of view is that the shop is offering teas and beach trays.

▲ **EASTCHURCH,** *The Village c1955* E153003

It is a fairly quiet day for traffic in Eastchurch, Sheppey. On the left is a shop advertising Coca-Cola and Lyons tea, and on the right is a garage and a café. Eastchurch has always had a link with aviation: the RAF had an aerodrome here, and the Royal Aero Club was based at Stanford Hill – it later became an open prison.

◄**EASTCHURCH**
The High Street c1955
E153011

The relief bus makes its way through Eastchurch High Street. In the village there is a memorial to two pioneers of aviation, Lord Brabazon and Charles Stewart Rolls.

▼ **EASTCHURCH,** *The Cliffs c1955* E153012

The cliffs and the area around Eastchurch are a haven for wildlife, and attract bird watchers and wildlife conservators from a wide area.

► **FOLKESTONE**
Park Hill Avenue and the Harvey Statue 1895 35528

The statue on the right is that of Dr William Harvey, the discoverer of the circulation of the blood, who was born in Folkestone in 1578. In the Folkestone museum there is a mortar and pestle used by Dr Harvey.

◄ FOLKESTONE
The View from the Leas 1906 53468

Folkestone pier can be seen on the right-hand side. It was built in 1887, but a fire in 1945 reduced it to smouldering debris and in 1952 it was demolished. The Leas shelter on the left was built in 1894; later a new building replaced the shelter, and in July 1927 the first concert was held in the Leas Cliff Hall.

► FOLKESTONE
The Leas 1918 68125

The Leas was connected to Lower Leas by a zigzag path, and by a water-balanced cliff lift which was opened in 1885.

FOLKESTONE
*The Leas Bandstand
1901* 48053

The Leas bandstand was built in 1885. A large crowd has gathered to hear the band, including the lady in the invalid carriage in the centre of the photograph. Further on, people are promenading. When Folkestone was one of the top seaside resorts, people of fashion would stay at the resort and parade in the morning so as to see and be seen.

FOLKESTONE, *The Stade 1912* 65006

This was the fishing area of Folkestone: note the fishing nets on the right-hand side by the steps. At the top of the buildings are pulleys for lifting items into the buildings of fish merchant F Pearson, whose fish boxes are probably the ones stacked outside.

FOLKESTONE
The View from the Pier 1918 68133

The large building at the rear of the beach was a swimming establishment - it included a swimming pool, a plunge bath, a saloon, assembly rooms and refreshment rooms. A large crowd has gathered on the beach to watch the rowers. Behind them is the Marine Studio, ready to take photographs of the holidaymakers.

FOLKESTONE, *The Leas and the War Memorial 1927* 80384

The war memorial was erected in 1922 and unveiled by the Earl of Radnor CIE, CBE, TS on December 1922.

FOLKESTONE, *Sunbathing c1950* F35012

There are plenty of changing tents on this beach, where a group
of boys wave at the camera (centre foreground). Folkestone was
popular with authors: Charles Dickens rented a property here
while writing *Little Dorrit*, and H G Wells lived at Spade House
while he wrote *Kipps* and *The History of Mr Polly*.

FOLKESTONE
Cockles and Whelks c1960 F35156

No day out was complete at the seaside without trying some local cockles, whelks or jellied eels. The paper bags hanging on this stall carried the slogan 'Our Motto: Service, Civility, Cleanliness!'.

FOLKESTONE, *Lower Landgate Road Toll Gate 1927* 80387

A car at the toll gate waits as the gate is opened; the gatekeeper's house is adjacent to the gates. The Channel Tunnel link from Folkestone to mainland France was started in the 1880s, and then abandoned. It was attempted again in 1973. At last on 6 May 1994 Her Majesty Queen Elizabeth II opened the tunnel that linked Britain with France. The Queen travelled on a Eurostar train through the tunnel, to be met by President Mitterand and other VIPs at Calais.

FOLKESTONE, *The Harbour c1960* F35159

Folkestone has always maintained a strong fishing community, which worked alongside the ferries when they operated out of Folkestone. Note the cranes in the background. The boat on the left is the *Susannah*.

GREATSTONE-ON-SEA
Sand Dunes c1955
G214003

During the days of smuggling the sand dunes offered good cover for those engaged in the trade. In later times the guests at Madison Holiday Camp would enjoy the sands of Romney Bay.

GREATSTONE-ON-SEA, *The Beach c1955* G214014

The road between Greatstone and Dungeness consists mainly of bungalows with the miniature railway running behind them, and the area can be pretty bleak in the winter. In the summer, holiday camps were busy, such as the Romney Sands Holiday Village where the railway stopped.

51

▼ **GREATSTONE-ON-SEA,** *Sand Dunes c1955* G214015

The sand dunes and beach make Greatstone the ideal place for families. It has safe bathing and plenty of space for ball games. One drawback is the wind, which can spoil a picnic and blow beach balls out of sight.

► **GREATSTONE-ON-SEA**
Coast Drive c1955
G214017

The aptly named Dune Tea Rooms is next to the post office at Greatstone, a popular place for families as it does not get as busy as some resorts. As it is very flat, the area is also a boon for cyclists.

◄ **HERNE BAY**
The Clock Tower and Tower Gardens 1897
40151

The long seafront at Herne Bay is dominated by the 80ft clock tower presented to the town in 1837, the year of Queen Victoria's accession. On the right is the Dolphin Hotel, one of the many town hotels that catered for visitors.

► **HERNE BAY**
The View from the Pier c1955 H75007

It would not be possible to take this photograph today, as the pier was destroyed by storms in 1979. However, there are plans to try and build another pier, which were put forward in 2003.

▼ **HERNE BAY,** *The Promenade c1955* H75013

In February 1953 the Promenade was buried under thousands of tons of shingle, and the roads blocked by smashed boats. All this was caused by the worst floods the county had known, when a tidal surge broke through the sea defences.

► **HYTHE**
The School of Musketry 1890 25891

The School of Musketry was later called the Small Arms School. As a military establishment it was started in 1807 to accommodate 300 men. It closed in 1968.

◄ **HYTHE**
The Parade 1899
44784

Hythe was once one of the Cinque Ports, and a very busy one, but the sea receded and the quay ended up half a mile inland. The town became a holiday resort; when this photograph was taken, people were taking a stroll along the West Parade, while the braver ones could change in the tents and have a dip in the water.

► **HYTHE**
The Royal Military Canal 1899 44786

The Royal Military Canal was created in 1807, at a time when Napoleon's Grande Armee was at Boulogne and a threat to Britain. The canal was intended to act as a defence against invasion.

55

▲ **HYTHE**
The Royal Military Canal 1918
68157

As the canal was never needed as a
defence, it became a haven for wildlife. It
was (and is) also used for leisure pursuits:
people hired boats to row on the canal,
and fishermen cast from the banks. A
water carnival takes place on the canal
every year with many decorated floats.

▶ **HYTHE,** *The Church 1918* 68162

St Leonard's parish church is an ancient
one: parts of the building date from 1100.
It was enlarged in 1165, and the tower
was added in 1750. In the crypt are
hundreds of skulls arranged on shelves. A
bomb dropped in the churchyard in May
1917 and killed the verger, Daniel Lyth.
Buried in the churchyard is Lionel Lukin,
the inventor of the lifeboat.

HYTHE
The High Street c1955 H141026

The old town of Hythe was first granted a charter in AD732 by King Ethelred. There was not too much traffic when this photograph was taken. On the left by Great Conduit Street is the National Provincial Bank, and further down is The White Hart public house, which dates from 1648. On the right-hand side is Fendall's wine and spirit stores.

HYTHE, *The High Street c1955* H141054

In the distance in the centre of this photograph is the sign for The King's Head public house, which in 1583 was known as The George, and later as The Sun. On the corner of Douglas Street is a grocery store (left). Note the blinds down on the shops on the right.

▶ **HYTHE**
*The Sutherland
House Hotel
c1960* H141075

Sutherland House
Hotel in Slade Street
was a private hotel;
Mrs Mary Goslett was
the proprietress.
Many retired colonial
civil servants and
military officers
would come to live in
these private hotels.

◀ **HYTHE**
The Beach c1960
H141080

Hythe had its own
lifeboat, but owing to the
difficulty of launching it
on Hythe beach, the
lifeboat house was built
on the boundary with
Sandgate. In the 1920s it
was said that 'early
summer and autumn are
the best times for visiting
Hythe, and persons with
pulmonary complaints or
dyspepsia are generally
benefited here.'

▲ **ISLE OF GRAIN,** *The Cat and Cracker Hotel c1955* I52001

The Cat and Cracker got its name in 1954, when the brewers Style & Winch Ltd of Maidstone named it after the catalytic cracker, which breaks down crude oil, and was used by the nearby Anglo-Iranian oil refinery. Note the toddler on the tricycle (centre).

◄**ISLE OF GRAIN**
The Beach c1955 I52008

Here on the beach at the Isle of Grain smugglers would land their booty to be transported to London. Behind the beach are concrete anti-tank defences, left over from World War II.

KINGSDOWN, *Upper Street 1918* 68504a

These 18th-century cottages were built to house farm workers and
fishermen when the latter moved up from the shore. The village
still has a peaceful and quiet air about it, though the narrow
streets can cause problems with traffic in the holiday season.

KINGSDOWN
The View from Cliff Walk 1924 76084

To the right of this view are the ranges used by the Royal Marines, who were based in Deal until 1996. Lower Kingsdown can be seen by the beach. At one time this area of Kingsdown had five shops and three pubs. The large field behind the flagpole is now used by the Scouting movement, and is always full of tents in the summer.

KINGSDOWN, *The Village and the Church 1924* 76085

The church of St John the Evangelist on the right was built in 1850 at a cost of £4500. Many of the houses seen here are built from flint and stone and salvaged ships' timbers.

► **KINGSDOWN**
*The White Cliffs
and the Dover
Patrol Memorial
1924* 76096

One of the most
pleasant walks over
the white cliffs is from
Kingsdown past the
golf course and up to
the Dover Patrol
Monument, then on
to St Margaret's Bay.
Cliff falls make it
dangerous to walk on
the beach.

◄ **KINGSDOWN**
*The Holiday Camp,
The Horse Shoe
c1955* K26049

The buildings in this
photograph have now all
been replaced by A-frame
Scandinavian wood
chalets, and the site has a
club room, swimming
pool and tennis courts. It
is very popular with
holidaymakers from
Europe because of its
nearness to Dover.

▲ **KINGSGATE,** *The Castle 1894* 34192a

Kingsgate takes its name from a gate erected to commemorate the landing of King Charles II and his brother the Duke of York on 13 June 1683.

◄ **KINGSGATE**
The Castle 1908 60381

Kingsgate Castle was rebuilt in the mid 1800s by Lord Holland. It was a private house for a while, and then became a hotel run by the North Foreland Hotels Ltd. One well known resident of Kingsgate was the actor Jack Warner, who played the policeman Dixon of Dock Green on television for 21 years, He died in 1981.

▶ **LEYSDOWN-ON-SEA**
The Beach c1955
L326015

In 1923 Leysdown proposed to change its name to Leysdown-Super-Mare, as it was becoming very busy with holiday camps, camping sites, and hotels, and more houses were being built to meet the needs of visitors. It is still Leysdown-on-Sea, however.

◀ **LEYSDOWN-ON-SEA**
Warden Point c1955
L326021

Since 1840, landslides have caused the loss of two parish churches in this area of Sheppey; an inn and some cottages have also ended up under the sea.

▲ **LEYSDOWN-ON-SEA,** *Station Road c1955* L326029

Leysdown is the most easterly village of the Isle of Sheppey. On the left is the Leysdown post office with a post box outside, while on the right is a motor-cycle with a side-car, which was a very common mode of transport at that time.

◄**LEYSDOWN-ON-SEA**
Warden Bay Caravan Park c1955 L326048

The Warden Bay Caravan Park also had chalets, which we can just see at the top right of the photograph. Note the 5mph speed limit sign just inside the narrow gates. The Sheppey light railway opened in 1901, and ran between Queensborough and Leydown; it closed in 1950, which upset many locals and holidaymakers.

◄LITTLESTONE-ON-SEA
The Parade c1955
L327019

To give the patients the benefit of the healthy sea breezes, a convalescent home for women and girls, with a wing for mothers and infants, was built in Nether Avenue in 1902. It contained 45 beds and 5 cots. It cost £6000 and was called Littlestone Convalescent Home. The sandy beach stretched for miles in each direction, and the seafront road ran for two miles.

◄ **LITTLESTONE-ON-SEA**
The Parade c1955 L327017

Littlestone became a popular residential resort in the 1890s. The seafront Grand Hotel was opened in 1891 on the Parade. A golf course was laid out in 1888 with an 18-hole and a 9-hole course, with a ladies' and a gentlemen's clubhouse.

▲ **LYDD,** *All Saints' Church c1955* L333013

The registers of All Saints date from 1542, but parts of the building originate from an early Saxon church. The building was extensively altered in 1887; it was damaged by a bomb in 1940, and then rebuilt in 1958.

◄ **LYDD**
The Air Terminal Buildings, Ferryfield Airport c1955 L333034

Ferryfield airport replaced the Lympne airport which the airline Silver City had been using since 1948. In that time 54,000 cars had been carried abroad.

LYDD
Ferryfield Airport c1955
L333030

The airport opened in July 1954. Flights were to Le Touquet, France and Ostend, Belgium, taking passengers and cars. The short flights enabled drivers to be on the roads of France or Belgium much more quickly than if they used the ferries.

MARGATE, *Newgate Gap Bridge 1890* 27442

Below Newgate Gap Bridge, on the right hand side, was Charlotte Pettman's original sea water baths, and she claimed that her bathing machines were far superior to any others. Donkeys could be hired here for strolls along the sandy beaches.

MARGATE
The Jetty and the Cliffs 1892 31442

Margate has nine miles of sandy beaches, which have made it a Mecca for day trippers and holidaymakers. The low cliffs and numerous caves were used by smugglers. In this photograph a horse stands on the beach, and another horse with a cart stands close to the cliff. Perhaps they were clearing seaweed, or just keeping the beach clean.

MARGATE, *The Parade 1897* 39578s

The clock tower on the right was erected in 1889 to commemorate Queen Victoria's Jubilee. The Dreamland Amusement Park opened in 1905, and has attracted thousands of people over the years. It has a Grade II listed roller coaster ride. The Amusement Park closed in 2003.

▼ **MARGATE,** *The Jetty and the Fort 1897* 39580s

The Promenade and jetty was built in the 1800s. In 1964 the jetty was badly damaged by fire; then in 1978 the severe weather destroyed most of it, and the lifeboat station was left marooned 500 yards out to sea.

▶ **MARGATE**
Marine Parade 1908
60364s

The lifeboat memorial on the right commemorates the crew of the surf boat *Friend of All Nations* which capsized on 2 December 1897 with the loss of nine lives. It was at Margate that the first bathing machines were invented in 1753.

◀ **MARGATE**
The Queen's Highcliffe Hotel 1927 80355

Known as the Queen's Highcliffe Hotel (Isle of Thanet Hotels Ltd), this was situated at Queen's Gardens, Cliftonville. The company also owned the Grand, also at Cliftonville.

▶ **MINSTER**
The Abbey Church and the Abbey Gate c1955
M373014

The abbey was founded in AD670 as a nunnery by Sexburga, widow of Ercombert, King of Kent; the original building was burnt by the Danes. Around 1130 the Archbishop of Canterbury restored the abbey and the church. In 1539, Henry VIII dissolved the abbey; all that remains today are the church of St Mary and St Sexburga, and the abbey gatehouse. The clock above the church door is inscribed with the words 'My times are in thy hand'.

▼ **MINSTER,** *The High Street c1955* M373018

In the distance in the centre of this photograph is The King's Arms public house; at this time it was one of the houses of the Maidstone brewers Style & Winch Ltd. The pub gets its name from a time when owners liked to show loyalty to the crown. On the corner is Uneeda hairdressing salon (centre), and above that an advertisement reads 'George Ramuz & Co for houses and land'.

► **MINSTER**
The Beach, Scrapsgate c1955 M373024

A mile north of Minster is Scrapsgate. Note the beach huts (left). As well as using them to change in, holidaymakers could boil a kettle for a cup of tea, and they could also store their deckchairs and other beach paraphernalia in them. These beach huts have become very sought-after today, and change hands for quite a lot of money.

◄ **MINSTER**
The High Street
c1960 M373032

Minster on the Isle of Sheppey has two public houses in its High Street, as we can see here: The King's Arms is on the left, and The Highlander in the centre. On the right-hand side is Robertson's the tobacconist and newsagent, advertising *The Daily Mail*. The word Sheppey is Saxon for 'sheep island'.

► **MINSTER**
Scrapsgate Bay
c1955 M373041

This family seem determined to make the most of their time at the seaside and contemplate the sea. The children seem less happy, one lying down and the other trying to keep the wind out. Note the beach huts on the right-hand side.

NEW ROMNEY, *Composite Postcard c1955* N141015

On this composite postcard of New Romney, we have the Dungeness lighthouse, built in 1904, and the Romney and Hythe District Light Railway, which started in 1927. The town of New Romney was once a powerful Cinque Port with strong smuggling links. St Nicholas' Church, New Romney, dates from the 12th century.

PEGWELL, *The Cliffs 1907* 58303

St Augustine landed here in AD597, and a St Augustine cross and well can be found at Cliffsend. At Ebbsfleet in Pegwell Bay there is a spot thought to be where Hengist and Horsa landed, signalling the beginning of the Anglo-Saxon, Jutish and Danish occupation of Britain.

▼ **PEGWELL,** *The Danish Viking Ship 'Hugin' c1950* P20021

Pegwell Bay houses the replica Viking dragon-headed longship which was rowed and sailed from Denmark to Broadstairs to celebrate the 1500th anniversary of the landing of Hengist and Horsa; it arrived on 28 July 1949.

► **PEGWELL**
The Cliffs 1918 68477

In 1966 a small hovercraft ran a service to Calais or pleasure trips to the Goodwin Sands from Pegwell Bay. Ramsgate International Hoverport, opened by Prince Philip in 1968, operated from Pegwell Bay, and from here the company Hover-Lloyd operated a service to Calais. Later all hovercraft crossings were moved to Dover.

◀ **PEGWELL**
The Convalescent Home 1907 58301

The Working Men's Club Union Convalescent Home at Pegwell Bay had a Mrs M E Boyland as superintendent, and B T Hall as secretary. The main hotel at Pegwell Bay was The Belle Vue, run by William Shaw.

▶ **QUEENSBOROUGH**
The Slipway c1955
Q4002

Queensborough gained its name in 1366, when Edward III gave the borough and port to his Queen Philippa. It once boasted a castle, but this was destroyed by Cromwell. A ferry service once operated from here to Holland.

▼ **QUEENSBOROUGH,** *High Street c1955* Q4004

On the right is an Ind Coope pub, The Old House at Home, a landmark for bargees on the River Medway. The pub had been rebuilt in 1914 and had been in the family of Captain Ruthvens for 102 years. Further on is The Castle Inn, and also in the High Street were The Ship, The Rose Inn, and The Ordnance Arms. It must have been thirsty work on the barges.

► **QUEENSBOROUGH**
Kingsferry Bridge
c1960 Q4025

Princess Marina opened this, the first rising platform bridge to be built for 25 years, on 13 April 1960. It replaced the old bridge that linked the Isle of Sheppey to the mainland.

◄ RAMSGATE
The Beach c1880
12731

In the centre of this photograph is the rail terminus of the line from Faversham. Opened in 1863, it closed in 1926 when a new station for the town was opened to the rear of the town. Note the wheeled stalls on the beach, and the row of chairs all in a line.

► RAMSGATE
The Pier
Lighthouse 1901
48035

A fine three-masted sailing ship is anchored behind the lighthouse. Plans for Ramsgate harbour were drawn up in 1750, and the harbour was extended in 1818.

RAMSGATE
The Beach 1907 58272

Here we see a very busy Ramsgate beach. To the left there is a beach hut inscribed 'The Crown Hotel': it would appear that the hotel had their own area of beach for changing on, or for serving drinks perhaps. On the right is Promenade Pier, erected in 1881. It was 555ft long and had a scenic railway on it; the pier was demolished in 1931.

▼ **RAMSGATE,** *Victoria Parade 1901* 48039

Some of Ramsgate's best hotels, such as The Casa Blanca and The Glanville, were on Victoria Parade, and they offered the guests the opportunity to walk out of the hotel and promenade along the Parade.

▶ **RAMSGATE**
The Pavilion from the Pier 1906 53467

The obelisk behind the Pavilion (left) commemorates the embarkation of George IV for Hanover in 1821. He decreed that Ramsgate harbour could use the prefix 'Royal'. The Royal Victoria Pavilion on Harbour Parade could seat 2000 people. Note the advertisement for Bailey's Pharmacy at 9 Queen Street (centre left).

RAMSGATE
The Quay and the Inner Harbour 1918 68467

A charabanc is parked by the harbour, bringing trippers to Ramsgate for pleasure cruises. In front of it another vehicle from Minster has unloaded its passengers. A yacht marina was opened in 1965 that could hold 120 boats.

RECULVER
The Shop c1955
R14003

Reculver is situated five miles east of Herne Bay, and it is popular with holidaymakers. Seen here in the centre is the Municipal Camping Ground, and the shop on the right is busy selling groceries, provisions, bread, and cakes, as well as newspapers, tobacco, and cigarettes to campers. On the left-hand side, milk crates are piled up awaiting collection.

▶ **RECULVER**
The Beach c1955
R14006

In March 1943, one mile to the east of Reculver Towers was cordoned off, and on 11 April Wing Commander Guy Gibson tested the Barnes Wallis 'bouncing bomb' in Reculver Bay. The Twin Towers were chosen as the release point for the bombs, as they resembled the towers at the Mohne and Eder dams in Germany. The dams were successfully attacked by Gibson and 617 Squadron on 16 May 1943, using the Barnes Wallis 'bouncing bomb' tested at Reculver. Wing Commander Gibson won the Victoria Cross following the raid.

◀ **RECULVER**
The Towers c1955
R14014

It is believed that in AD43 the Romans under Emperor Claudius set up a small initial camp at Reculver because of its safe harbour. The Romans built a fortress here called Regulbium, and in the 12th century a church was built inside the fortress.

▲ **RECULVER,** *The Towers 1892* 31457

Known as 'The Sisters', the towers are all that remain of St Mary's Church - it was blown up in 1809 to stop it falling into the sea. The towers were purchased by Trinity House in 1810 as an aid to navigation. From 1925 the towers were looked after by the Ministry of Works, and a lot of money was spent to prevent them falling into the sea.

◀ **RECULVER**
The King Ethelbert Public House c1955 R14015

The name of this Whitbread pub, the King Ethelbert, is in remembrance of the Saxon king who ruled Kent from AD560-616. Part of the pub is built on an old Roman fort. Nearby there is a caravan site.

▶ **SANDGATE**
General View 1892
29954

Sandgate Castle, built
in 1573, was so altered
in 1806 to make a
defence against the
feared invasion by
Napoleon that it
resembled the
Martello towers built
along the coast (see
centre of photograph).

◀**SANDGATE**
Shorncliffe 1903
50365

Shorncliffe Military
Camp was re-established
in 1854 to become one of
the most important
military bases in the
country. The barracks
overlooked the town and
sea. Note the house
under construction on
the right-hand side.

▲ **SANDGATE,** *The Beach 1906* 56946

The fishing off Sandgate was very good, with catches of plaice, codling, conger, and pouting the most common. During World War II the whole beach was covered in obstacles and coils of barbed wire to help prevent an invasion.

◀**SANDGATE**
The Esplanade looking East 1906 56949

Sandgate has become a suburb of Folkestone. On a good day the coast of France can be seen clearly from the Sandgate Esplanade. Note the ornate street light and the lady's fancy parasol.

▼ **SANDGATE,** *Radnor Cliff 1906* 56957

Sandgate lies a mile west of Folkestone. Radnor Cliff was where many of the town's wealthy residents lived; here their houses overlook the beach, where a naval man appears to be getting his boat ready for sailing.

▶ **SANDGATE**
The Convalescent Home 1906 56959

Beach House Convalescent Home was built in 1890; it was open to men, women and children from all parts of the kingdom, and was supported by the London Samaritan Society.

◀**SANDGATE**
The Memorial and the High Street c1960 S55036

The memorial marks the spot where a bomb exploded during a German air raid on 25 May 1917. The cross commemorates all the men from the parish who fell during the Great War 1914-1918. To the right is the Sandgate Newsagency, followed by Stace the bookseller and the Swiss Miss Café.

▶ **SANDWICH**
The River Stour 1914 67158

To the left of the River Stour is the Bell Hotel; the town records report that the mayor 'presented King Charles II with a glass of sack at the Bell tavern door' when his Majesty rode in with the Duke of York and Prince Rupert in 1669. The King accepted the drink on horseback.

▲ SANDWICH
The Barbican 1914 67159

On the left of this photograph of the Barbican is the Crispin Inn – St Crispin was the patron saint of cobblers and shoemakers. Opposite is a garage, and on the wall is an advertisement for Rigden & Son, Decorators and Plumbers.

▶ SANDWICH
St Peter's Church 1914 67160

St Peter's Church was built between 1200-1210 on the site of an earlier structure. The two shops in the photograph are (from the left) a watchmaker's and a jeweller's, and the shop with the bicycle leaning outside is a butcher's.

SANDWICH
The Weavers c1955
S60016

To the left is the sign for the Whitbread pub The Three Kings, which was entered through the wide arch; then a Georgian door led to a private bar and 'snug', which resembled a scene from a Dickens novel. Unfortunately, the pub closed in 1970. The Weavers (the old timber-framed building) recalls the days when Sandwich was the centre of the immigrant Flemish weaving industry.

SANDWICH, *The Barbican c1955* S60019

The Barbican was built during the reign of Henry VIII. All traffic to Thanet passed under its arches, where a toll was paid. The Admiral Owen pub through the arch was originally a 16th-century inn; it was re-named after Admiral Owen, who destroyed French gunboats off Boulogne in 1840.

▼ **SANDWICH,** *The Barbican c1955* S60018

Sandwich was an original thriving Cinque Port, but today the sea is two miles away. Through the arch The Admiral Owen pub is advertising Trumans Beer.

► **SHEERNESS**
The Beach c1950 S528001

Sheerness on the Isle of Sheppey was an important naval centre from 1665 until the navy left in 1960. At Garrison Point a grandstand view of shipping in the Thames estuary can be seen.

◄ **SHEERNESS**
High Street c1950
S528007

There are more bicycles than cars in this 1950s view of Sheerness High Street. Note the numerous tobacco advertisements on the left for Players Navy Cut, Wills Gold Flake and Wills Star cigarettes. Further down the road a lot of people are gathered outside Woolworth's store - perhaps they had a sale on.

► **SHEERNESS**
High Street c1950
S528009

In the centre of this photograph is the Royal Hotel, a Victorian building that used to advertise itself as a 'Family and Commercial Hotel, fully licensed, premier position, garage'. Behind it is the Rio cinema - it closed in 1958. On the left is Sheerness and District Co-operative Society, with a ladies' and gentlemen's hairdressing salon next door.

▲ SHEERNESS
The Beach c1955 S528027

It was to Sheerness dockyard that Nelson's body was brought, preserved in a barrel of spirit, following his death at Trafalgar. Here in much happier times a pleasure boat returns passengers to the shore, and in the background we can see a big wheel pleasure ride.

► SHEERNESS
The Clock Tower c1955 S528035

The clock tower was built to celebrate the coronation of King Edward VII. Behind the clock is Boots the chemist.

SHORNCLIFFE
The Married Men's Quarters 1903 50399

The Shorncliffe camp has played host to many regiments and units since 1854. Many soldiers marched from these barracks in 1914 to embark at Folkestone for France, many fated never to return. On the wall of the end house is a birdcage hanging outside.

ST MARGARET'S AT CLIFFE, *Portal House 1898* 40818

The National Deposit Friendly Society Convalescent Home, Portal House, was run by a matron, Miss Sherman, and was one of several convalescent homes on the Kent coast.

▲ **ST MARGARET'S AT CLIFFE**
The Cliffe Hotel 1903 50407

The Cliffe Hotel was a very popular hotel in Victorian days. Today the village and bay are looked after by the St Margaret's Bay Trust, who were formed in 1970; they have created the Pines Gardens, a community centre, and a youth club.

▶ **ST MARGARET'S AT CLIFFE**
The Parish Church, the West Door 1918 68495

The church of St Margaret's is a Norman church. The tower was restored in 1866. The register dates from 1588, and the church can seat 469 people.

▲ ST MARGARET'S BAY
1891 29679

One could not be any nearer the sea than when you stayed at the Lanzarote Boarding House, the large building on the right of the photograph. To the left are the winding steps from the cliff top to the beach.

◄ ST MARGARET'S BAY
Up the Steps 1908 60349

With the cliffs rising up to 400 feet, visitors would have been glad of these steps to get from the village to the beach.

ST MARGARET'S BAY
Looking West 1918 68488

Many prominent people came to St Margaret's Bay to
stay at the Granville Hotel, now long gone. Others to
have homes here were Noel Coward and Ian Fleming.
Most of the houses on the beach were destroyed by
shelling in World War II.

ST MARGARET'S BAY
The Dover Patrol Memorial 1924 76098

The Dover Patrol Memorial base stone was laid by HRH
Prince Arthur of Connaught KG on 19 November 1910,
and the memorial was unveiled by HRH The Prince of
Wales KG on 27 July 1921. Inscribed on the base is: 'To
the glory of God and in everlasting remembrance of the
Dover Patrol 1914-1918, they died that we may live, may
we be worthy of their sacrifice.' Another later inscription
reads: 'To the memory of the officers and men of the
Royal Navy and Merchant service who gave their lives
sailing the waters of the Dover Strait 1939-1945.'

ST MARGARET'S BAY
The Beach 1924 76102

On the beach at
St Margaret's Bay stood
The Green Man public
house; this was another
building that was destroyed
by the shelling in World War
II, but it was rebuilt, and
now trades as the
Coastguard. It is the nearest
pub to France.

ST MARGARET'S BAY, *The Zigzag Path 1924* 76103

When taking the cliff top walk from Kingsdown to St Margaret's Bay, we can reach the beach via the Zigzag path, whose steps enable us to descend easily.

▼ **ST MARGARET'S BAY,** *The South Foreland Lighthouse 1924* 76104

The lighthouse gained fame when Marconi conducted the first ship to shore radio experiments here in 1898. Today a popular walk is the one to the lighthouse.

▶ **ST MARY'S BAY**
The Children's Holiday Camp c1960 S538026

The Duke of York, later King George VI, founded holiday camps like this one at St Mary's Bay, where a mixture of children from slum areas and from wealthy parents could come together. During the holidays the Duke would arrive and in shirt sleeves and shorts would join in the games.

◀ **ST MARY'S BAY**
The Beach c1955
S538004

One famous resident of St Mary's Bay was the authoress Edith Nesbit, who wrote *The Railway Children*; she lived with her husband Captain Tucker at The Long Boat until she died in 1924. She loved St Mary's Bay, the marshes and the beach. The beach was another place for smugglers to unload their goods. Then they would take the contraband into the Romney Marshes, that they knew so much better than the Revenue Men.

▶ **ST MARY'S BAY**
The Miniature Train leaving the Station c1960 S538043

This miniature mainline railway opened in July 1927, running between Hythe and New Romney. A year later it was extended to Dungeness. Seen here is Hurricane, a locomotive one-third of the size of normal engines.

► **SWALECLIFFE**
*The Shopping
Centre, Seaview
Holiday Camp
c1955* S545008

Swalecliffe is two miles
east of Whitstable and
a popular area for
holidaymakers. Here
campers queue up at
the camp shop for their
daily newspaper, milk,
bread and so on. Three
other campers enjoy
the pleasure of riding a
four-wheeled cycle.

◄ **SWALECLIFFE**
*Seaview Holiday
Camp c1955* S545019

In the days before
package holidays abroad
were so easily available,
this type of holiday
camp was very popular
for the working classes.
Although the buildings
were little more than
garden sheds, the sea air
and other facilities on
the sites made up for
any discomforts.

▲ **TANKERTON,** *The Slopes c1955* T228066

Tankerton adjoins Whitstable to the east. It was developed by the Tankerton Estate Company, which was established in 1890. It had a pier which was opened in 1893, then demolished in 1913 as being no longer serviceable. The Embassy cinema on the right was opened as the Troc in 1931 and closed in 1950.

◄ **WALMER**
The Front 1892 31434

The Walmer Lifeboat Station on the right of this photograph was opened in 1856 and closed in 1912, but in 1927 it was reopened. The Stag Hotel, next to the tallest building in the centre, was a hotel under the control of the brewers Ash of Canterbury. The hotel advertised itself as facing the sea, 'drop in and have a wet'.

▼ **WALMER,** *The Promenade 1906* 56929

On the left of this photograph is a large winch: as neither Walmer nor Deal had a harbour, fishing boats had to be winched ashore. Today there is a cycle path alongside the promenade. Sir Arthur Wellesley, later the Duke of Wellington, lived in Castle Road in 1808, and later at Walmer Castle as Lord Warden of the Cinque Ports, where he died in 1852.

► **WALMER**
The Glen 1906 56934

Note the house being built on the left hand side. St Mary's Church (centre) was newly erected in 1887; it was built of Kentish rag and Bath stone. The tower was added in 1893. The old St Mary's Church dated from Norman times. Today, Glen Road leads to upper Kingsdown.

◄ **WALMER**
The Strand looking North 1924 76079

Wollaston Road leads off The Strand to the left. Next to it is the Boatman's Reading Room, the Strand Boot Stores, and the Walmer Stores. Today the Deal Memorial Bandstand stands on the green. It commemorates the eleven Royal Marine bandsmen killed by an IRA bomb at the Royal Marine School of Music, Deal, in September 1989.

▶ **WALMER**
The Strand 1924 76081

The Walmer Stores in the centre of this photo has its blinds down. It was a sad day for Walmer and Deal when on 22 March 1996 the Royal Marines beat a final retreat and ended a 300-year association with the towns. His Royal Highness Prince Philip, Captain General of the Royal Marines, said: 'I am very grateful for this opportunity to offer, on behalf of the Corps, our appreciation and gratitude to the people of Walmer and Deal for their support, tolerance and affection over so many years.' The Royal Marines were moved to Portsmouth.

WESTGATE ON SEA
The Cliffs 1907 58314

The very keen winds and sea at Westgate helped form caves in the chalk cliffs. Here is a fisherman with large net, plus a basket on his back for catch of fish or shrimps.

WESTGATE ON SEA, *St Mildred's Hotel and Baths 1907* 58317

St Mildred's Hotel frontage is laid out with gardens, lawns and a tennis court. The hotel's publicity said that its guests could take 'gentle activity'.

WESTGATE ON SEA
St Mildred's Bay
c1955 W280005

Westgate on Sea, with its sandy beaches, green lawns and flower beds, appeals to families who seek the quieter resort. The more lively Margate is only two miles away.

WESTGATE ON SEA, *The Hotels and the Beach 1890* 27463

Two of Westgate's leading hotels were the Beach House Hotel on the left, and the large St Mildred's Hotel and Bathing Establishment (centre). Note the children on the beach in their little sailor suits, and the picnic hamper.

▼ **WESTGATE ON SEA,** *Esplanade Gardens 1899* 44811

Two miles west of Margate, Westgate on Sea has two bays; sea walls built along the curves of the bays form two promenades with steps down to the beach, and gardens are laid out for the benefit of visitors.

► **WESTGATE ON SEA**
St Mildred's Bay 1907
58311

So popular was Westgate on Sea that it had a golf course, a cricket club and a lawn tennis club. In April 1915 land at a nearby farm was requisitioned for an airfield to defend the area against Zeppelin attacks. A flight of No 2 Squadron was based there.